The Caller

FASTBACK® Horror

The Caller

RICHARD LAYMON

GLOBE FEARON
Pearson Learning Group

FASTBACK® HORROR BOOKS

The Caller
The Disappearing Man
The Hearse
Live Bait
The Lonely One
The Masterpiece

The MD's Mistake
Night Games
Night Ride
No Power on Earth
The Rare Shell
Tomb of Horror

All photography © Pearson Education, Inc. (PEI) unless specifically noted.

Copyright © 2004 by Pearson Education, Inc., publishing as Globe Fearon®, an imprint of Pearson Learning Group, 299 Jefferson Road, Parsippany, NJ 07054. All rights reserved. No part of this book may be reproduced or transmitted in any form or by any means, electronic or mechanical, including photocopying, recording, or by any information storage and retrieval system, without permission in writing from the publisher. For information regarding permission(s), write to Rights and Permissions Department.

Globe Fearon® and Fastback® are registered trademarks of Globe Fearon, Inc.

ISBN 0-13-024512-7
Printed in the United States of America
1 2 3 4 5 6 7 8 9 10   07 06 05 04 03

1-800-321-3106
www.pearsonlearning.com

Cora jumped with surprise when the telephone rang. She knew that it couldn't be her cell phone since she had misplaced it in the move. She set the cinder block down on the plank that would serve as a bookshelf and turned around. It took her a moment to spot the phone resting atop a cardboard box in the corner of her new apartment. She hurried toward it, stepping around cartons and furniture.

What's the rush? she asked herself. Whoever is calling must surely have a wrong number. The phone had been put in just that afternoon, and so far she'd been too busy unpacking to let anyone know her new number.

She hoped the caller would hang up before she could reach the phone. No such luck. It was still ringing as she bent over the box and picked up the handset.

"Hello?" she asked.

"Hello." The man's voice didn't sound familiar.

"Who is this, please?"

"Who is this?" he asked.

She ignored his question. *No way,* she thought, *am I going to tell this guy my name.* "What number are you calling?"

"Yours," he said.

"I'm afraid you must have dialed the wrong number. Who were you trying to reach?"

"You."

"You don't even know who I am," she said, trying to keep her voice calm. Either the man was too confused to understand that he had reached a wrong number, or he was a crank. Maybe he got his kicks by phoning people at random. Cora chose to believe that he was simply confused. "This is 555-3765," she told him.

"I know," he said.

Cora sighed. "Look, I just got this phone today. Maybe the person you're trying to reach is the one who had this number before."

"You have a very nice voice."

Cora felt a tremor of fear. *He is a crank,* she thought. *My first caller in my brand new apartment, and he has to be a nut.* "Thanks," she muttered.

"I want to be your friend."
Without speaking another word, she hung up.

"Hello?"

"Hi Frank, it's Cora."

"What's wrong?"

"What makes you think something is wrong?"

"Because it's eleven o'clock at night, mostly. And you don't sound like your usual cheery self."

"Sorry. Did I wake you up?"

"No. What's the trouble? I hope you haven't changed your mind about going to the beach tomorrow."

"It's not that. I just wanted to let you know my new number." She read it to him from the plastic strip below the push buttons.

"Got it," Frank said. "But you didn't call me at this hour just to tell me your number. Feeling lonely? Got the Saturday night blues? All dressed up with nowhere to go?"

She smiled. "I do miss you," she said.

"You're the one who wouldn't go out tonight so you could unpack."

"I know. I'm feeling a little down, that's all. I just got a call from some nut who says I've got a nice voice and wants to be my friend. It spooked me a little."

"How did he get your number?"

"It beats me. He must have just dialed

the first thing that came into his head."

Frank said nothing for a few moments. When he spoke again, his voice sounded serious. "You didn't let him know your name or address, I hope."

"Are you kidding?"

"Well, as long as he doesn't know where to find you . . ."

"I know. It still makes me nervous, though. The fact that his *voice* can get to me."

"Unplug your phone."

"I might as well not have a phone, if I'm going to leave it unplugged. Besides, *you* might want to call me."

"True. Well, if he calls again, the best thing to do is not say a word. Just hang up. Guys who make nut calls want to hear something from the one on the other end.

He'll probably lose interest, real fast, if you don't talk to him."

"Fine. I'll give it a try."

"And don't worry. He's probably harmless. Guys like that are usually afraid of their own shadows. That's why they stay inside and make nice, safe calls to strangers."

"You seem to know a lot about it," Cora said, smiling.

"Is your refrigerator running?" he asked.

"Better go catch it!" they both said at once. Cora laughed along with him. "Crank," she said.

"You, too."

"Look, I'd better let you get your beauty sleep," she told him. "See you in the morning."

"If this guy . . . Don't be afraid to call me again if you get worried. Any hour. I'm as near as your phone."

"Right."

"And if you want me to come over now, just say the word."

"No, it's okay. I'll hang tough."

"That's my girl. Sleep tight."

"You, too."

With a feeling of calm, Cora said goodnight and set the phone down. As it clacked against its plastic cradle, the harsh blare of a sudden ringing sent a jolt through her.

Trembling, Cora stared at the telephone. The ringing had started the instant she'd hung up. Frank wouldn't have been able to dial her number that fast.

There is no law that says I have to answer it, she thought.

She stood stiffly beside the phone, watching it. The plastic looked bright and shiny, but as she gazed at it she could almost see the man at the other end. He sat in a dimly lighted, shabby little room. He held a grimy phone to his ear. His eyes were watery, and he stared blankly into space.

Hang up, she thought. *Leave me alone!*

But the phone kept ringing. Again and again, its bell rang, demanding an answer. Cora flinched each time it rang, then waited through seconds of silence hoping the caller would give up. He didn't give up. Frightened and angry, Cora finally picked up the phone. She held it to her ear and said nothing.

"Cora?"

She gasped. It was the voice of the stranger. And now he knew her name. Her voice shaking, she said, "Who is this?"

"I want to be your friend, but you're not being nice."

"How do you know my name?"

"I know more than you think. You shouldn't have hung up. That wasn't nice. I just wanted to talk to you."

"I don't want to talk to you."

"I'm lonely, Cora."

"That doesn't give you any right to bother me. A lot of people are lonely and don't go around making freaky calls in the middle of the night. If you don't leave me alone, I'll call the police."

"Oh no you won't," he said in a teasing voice. "I won't let you."

"I'd like to see you try and stop me," she snapped, and reached down toward the cradle, planning to push one of the cut-off buttons.

"Don't hang up or you'll be sorry," he said, his voice suddenly firm.

She gasped for air. She felt as if she'd been punched in the stomach. Her shaking finger stopped above the button.

"Yes, Cora, I can see you."

Whirling around, she gazed across the cluttered room at the picture window. It had no curtains. Reflected on the glass was a dim image of the nearby lamp and chair, the boxes on the floor. Beyond it, the night looked black.

He's out there, Cora thought.

"You're very pretty," he whispered into her ear. "I like to look at you. I want you to be my friend."

She slammed down the phone and rushed toward the window. A scream nearly leaped from her throat as a figure lurched into view. She slapped a hand across her mouth to stop the outcry—and so did the person in the window. "It's me," she said in a soft voice.

But he is out there somewhere, watching me.

Leaning across a chair, she turned off the lamp. Darkness fell over the room.

Now he can't see me, she told herself, and stepped up to the window. On the street corner three stories below was the pay telephone she had used a few times before her own phone was put in. Even though the booth was dark, someone could still be inside it. From down there, however, the man wouldn't be able to see into her apartment.

Across the street stood an eight story apartment building. Light shone from some of its windows, but most were dark.

He's watching me from one of the dark ones, Cora thought. *Maybe with a telescope. Maybe with a scope powerful enough to let him read my telephone number off the plastic strip. Is that possible?* she wondered. *But how else could he have learned my number?*

Unless he was here in the apartment.

The thought made an icy knot in her stomach.

He's not here now, she told herself. *I only had one phone put in. He's using his own phone. In his own apartment. Across the street. With his telescope trained on my window.*

As long as he doesn't know where to find you, Frank had said.

But he does!

Careful not to trip in the darkness, Cora made her way back across the floor. She had no trouble finding the phone. Its shiny plastic almost seemed to glow. But how could she dial Frank's number without turning on a light?

Kneeling beside the box, she picked up the handset. As the dial tone buzzed in her ear, she felt the one plastic button that was in the middle of the bottom row. She pushed it. A faint sound of ringing came to her ear.

"Operator," said a woman's voice.

"Yes. I'm blind. I'd like you to put through a call for me."

"Certainly."

She told Frank's number to the woman. She heard a series of beeps, then more ringing.

The ringing stopped.

"Mmmm?"

"Me again. I'm sorry if I woke you up, but you know that guy I told you about, that nut who called me? Well, he's watching me. He called me again and he threatened me and *he can see me*! I think he's in an apartment across the street. I'm scared, Frank. I know it's late and everything, but I want you to come over right away. Please. I'm afraid he might . . . come over."

"I only wanted to be your friend," said the voice on the phone.

"Frank! Did you hear that? He's on the line!"

"I'm on the line," the man said. "But Frank isn't."

"No!" she cried out.

"Oh yes. And I'm not happy with you, Cora. Didn't I warn you not to call for help?"

"How did you . . . ?" She shook her head. There was only one way he could have answered Frank's phone. He'd gone to Frank's apartment! Somehow, he'd found out where Frank lived, and gone there, and . . . "If you hurt Frank, you creep, I'll . . ."

"Oh, Frank's just fine."

"I want to talk to him."

"I don't want you to talk to him. I want you to talk to me."

"Put him on the phone, or I'm hanging up."

"Hanging up will do you no good, Cora."

"What do you want?"

"I want you to talk to me. I want you to be nice to me. I want you to be my friend. As I said, I'm lonely. I mean you no harm. I want to call you whenever I wish, just to chat."

"How often?" she asked, feeling defeated.

"Oh, once or twice a day. You may feel

free to talk about anything you wish. Tell me how your day went, or about books you may have read or movies you've seen. Talk to me about Frank, if you wish. I'm not the jealous type. Of course, I would like to know you better. I would like to hear such things as you might share with a very close friend—your joys and problems and fears."

"If I promise to do this, you won't hurt Frank?"

"I won't hurt Frank," he told her, "and I won't hurt you."

"All right," she said.

"Fine. Let's have our first chat right now. But first, turn on the lamp so I can see you better."

Cora frowned in confusion. He knew the

light was off. "You're not at Frank's!" she blurted, and slammed the phone down.

It rang again at once. She picked it up.

"Cora, we made a deal."

She flung the handset to the carpet. The voice still came faintly through the earpiece, sounding a long way off.

She reached around the base of the phone and grabbed the cord. Keeping it in her hand, she crawled along the floor, following it to the jack in the wall. She fought an urge to rip it loose. Carefully, she unplugged it.

"There you go, creep," she muttered into the darkness. "Try to call me now."

Standing up, she leaned against the wall. She gasped for breath as her heart thudded wildly.

He's just across the street, her mind warned. *What if he's crazy enough to come over?* She stared at the phone, wanting to plug it in and call Frank or the police.

He won't let me.

Somehow, he's in control of the phone.

But if he's on his way over, he won't be able to block my call.

Frank could get to her apartment in ten minutes. The police might even be faster. But what if the man got there first?

She couldn't risk it. Pushing herself away from the wall, she stepped past the telephone. She stopped at her door, frightened to open it. What if *he* was on the other side? No, it wasn't possible. Even if he left his room across the street as soon as she had pulled the plug, he couldn't be here yet.

She yanked open her door. Leaning out, she stared down the long hallway. She saw no one. The other apartment doors were all shut. If only she had lived here long enough to meet some of her neighbors! She knew she couldn't force herself to knock on a stranger's door. Not at this hour of the night.

He might not even be coming, she thought.

But she couldn't count on that. She had to get out.

She reached back to pull the door shut. The telephone rang.

Her hand froze on the knob.

It can't be ringing!

But it was.

I'm going crazy, she thought.

Whirling around, she felt along the dark wall until her finger found the switch. The overhead light came on. Her eyes darted to the long, white cord. It lay curled across the carpet like a dead snake. Still unplugged.

The phone rang again . . . and again.

Resting on the cardboard box, it shook as the bell rang inside it. The handset was on the floor where she'd dropped it.

This can't be happening, Cora thought.

She took a step backward.

The cord lashed out and whipped around her ankles. Before she could move, it yanked her feet out from under her. She hit the floor hard on her back. Raising her head, she saw the base of the phone leap from the box. She flung up her arms to protect her face. The phone slammed down on her belly, knocking the wind out of her. She grabbed it. But before she could throw it off, the handset crashed against the side of her head.

The blow made her dizzy and weak. Her arms dropped heavily to her sides.

The handset pushed against the side of her head, the earpiece tight against her ear, the mouthpiece pressed to her chin.

"I just wanted to be your friend," said the phone.

"Okay," she gasped.

"Too late."

The cord slid up her body. It felt cold and slick as it coiled around her neck.

"I'll do . . . whatever you want," she said.

"Too late."

The cord drew tight. She pulled at it. It was no use.

She heard quiet, hissing laughter in her ear.

She couldn't breathe.

But her legs, no longer bound by the cord, were free. Rolling over, she got to her hands and knees. The cord still choked her. The phone box stayed against her stomach as if clinging to her. "You can't get away," said the voice at her ear.

On her feet, she staggered across the floor. She grabbed the end of the cord. It flipped and twisted in her hand, but didn't pull free. The middle of the cord kept strangling her as she stumbled to the lamp. She knocked the shade off. With tingling, numb fingers, she twisted out the bulb. She turned the switch. She clutched the end of the phone cord with both hands and shoved it into the open bulb socket.

Sizzling and snapping, current shot up the cord. It tried to jerk free. The base pounded against her stomach. A horrible scream filled her ear. The phone started ringing, ringing without stopping. Threads of white smoke curled from the tiny holes of the mouthpiece. The cord around her neck jumped and squirmed, no longer choking her.

Suddenly, the phone went silent. The scream ended. So did the ringing. It fell away from her stomach. The cord yanked it to a stop. As it swayed in front of her knees, the handset dropped and bounced on the carpet.

Gasping for air, Cora unwrapped the cord from her neck.

She held the phone in her hands.

She stared at herself in the window for a moment, then hurled the telephone. It struck the glass, crashed through, and disappeared into the night.